IMAGES
of England

AROUND
ROTHWELL

Jawbones, c. 1904. These jawbones were knocked down by a car. They were replaced only to have the same thing happen again. The present jaw bones are situated on the other side of the road.

IMAGES
of England

AROUND
ROTHWELL

Compiled by
Simon Bulmer and Albert Brown

TEMPUS

First published 1999
Copyright © Simon Bulmer and Albert Brown, 1999

Tempus Publishing Limited
The Mill, Brimscombe Port,
Stroud, Gloucestershire, GL5 2QG

ISBN 0 7524 1802 5

Typesetting and origination by
Tempus Publishing Limited
Printed in Great Britain by
Midway Clark Printing, Wiltshire

*This book is dedicated to the memory of Jack Higgins and to the next generation,
particularly Charlotte, Leigh, Abigail, Ashley, Shaun and Mark;
they are the history makers of the future.*

Front cover: Rothwell Temperance Band, c. 1903.

Thatched cottages in Royds Green, *c.* 1900.

Contents

Acknowledgements

Simon and Albert would like to thank the following: Leeds City Council Archives, Bernard Bradley, Jim Hardwick, Marjory Clarkson, NCB, Stuart Earl, Robert Carrington, Rothwell Temperance Band, Rothwell and District Historical Society, Enid Bulmer and Hazel Aldam.

Simon would like to give special thanks to the following: Susan for putting up with my constant disappearances over the last months; Steve Burt whose enthusiasm for history is an inspiration; Albert Brown for opening his door to me over the last few months and sharing his great knowledge of Rothwell; and last, but not least, thanks to granddad for the gift of *The History of Rothwell* (Batty, 1877) without which none of this would have been possible. '*Tell me about the old days again granddad…*'

Springhead house, built in 1888. This was situated on the left hand side of the main entrance to Rothwell Park from Park Lane.

Introduction

Rothwell is an ancient settlement. Most historians who have written about the area seem to agree that it was first settled in Saxon times and yet it is an archaeological fact that at least one part of Rothwell was settled by a Roman garrison, in the fourth century. A Roman artefact – a stone coffin, containing the remains of a woman – was unearthed while making the cutting on Bell Hill in 1753. There was additionally the discovery of a Roman horseshoe during the digging of foundations for a brewery at Carlton Bridge in 1870. There is other evidence to suggest that Rothwell may have some connection with the ancient Celtic kingdom of Elmet from the seventh century. For example the naming of a lead well at Rothwell, possibly after the ancient district of Lead in the kingdom of Elmet. The first documentary evidence of Rothwell is contained within the Domesday Book, where it is recorded that Rothwell had a water corn mill, worth two shillings per annum, and an overall rateable valuation of eight pounds per annum.

After the conquest Ilbert de Lacy was given a vast tract of land stretching from Pontefact to Blackburn in Lancashire by his king, William Duke of Normandy, better known as William the Conqueror. This land known as the honor of Pontefract was given to Ilbert for his services to the King in helping to defeat the men of the West Riding of Yorkshire and all the lands between Pontefract and Blackburn. It was within the Honor of Pontefract that Rothwell lay. It was used as a royal hunting park surrounded by a palisade fence seven miles in length said to enclose an area of approximately two square miles, stocked with deer, wild boar and other animals of the chase. There was also a royal hunting lodge fit to house the King of England, his courtiers and the soldiers of his personal bodyguard when he hunted at Rothwell. King John stayed at Rothwell on several occasions in the thirteenth century as did Edward II in the fourteenth century. Ilbert de Lacy died around 1087 leaving the lands to his son Robert. Through a long succession of de Lacies the land finally became part of the crown properties in the fourteenth century in the reign of Edward III.

Edward III gave his wife Queen Phillipa a part of the Honor of Pontefract and the other to his son John of Gaunt. On the death of Queen Phillipa the land passed to Henry Earl of Lancaster. John of Gaunt married Blanche – Henry's daughter – and when Henry died the lands became one again under John of Gaunt. The legend of John of Gaunt is still told today in Rothwell, it is said that he killed the last wild boar on Styebank.

It was John of Gaunt's son Henry Bolingbrook, later to become Henry IV, who granted the status of a market town to Rothwell, 'on a Wednesday forever to be holden' in the words of the charter of 1408. Afterwards a market cross of local stone was erected in the middle of the King's highway on the hill top at the head of the main street of Rothwell. It stood in the same place for more than 500 years until it was unfortunately demolished in a road accident. It has been replaced by a modern precast concrete structure and re-erected some twelve metres from its original position.

The parish of Rothwell has a long history of coal mining An archaeological discovery within the parish in the nineteenth century, at Lofthouse, found coal ashes, broken coinage moulds and traces of silver waste. This indicated that Romans mined and used coal in the area in the fourth century. The 1341 extent of Rothwell records 'John the Collier' living at Oulton. The 1425 valuation of Rothwell records the story of Simon Symeon a soldier of fortune, to whom (it is said) John of Gaunt gave a parcel of land at Rothwell and the right to dig carborundum (coal). Furthermore a map of Rothwell in 1530 shows the way to the pits. The Duchy records for the Honor of Pontefract, written in the thirty-second year of the reign of Elizabeth I records that Mr Bland of Carlton paid five pounds annually to the Queen for the right to dig coal on the moor of Lofthouse. A magistrate order from the bench at Wakefield, dated 1610, records the damage done by the large number of horses and carts going to the pit to fetch coal. These were using the King's highway between the market towns of Leeds and Wakefield. At the end of that century coals were being conveyed on the backs of asses or donkeys from the pits at Ardsley and Middleton across Rothwell Haigh down to the coal staiths on the side of the River Aire, at Woodlesford. Through the eighteenth and nineteenth centuries coal mining was a major source of employment in Rothwell parish. This lasted well into the twentieth century before the total demise of the industry in the area, leaving virtually no evidence that pits existed in the area with coal mining at Rothwell becoming just a memory of the past.

Modern Rothwell and its surrounding areas have lost many industries of the past such as coal mining, rope and twine making, woollen mills and farming. Since the abolition of Rothwell Urban District Council in 1974 Rothwell has been administered by Leeds City Council. The community was thus robbed of its individual identity and nowadays it seems to be just another part of the urban sprawl of the growing city of Leeds.

Many of Rothwell's historical buildings have been demolished over several decades of slum clearances, both in the centre and outlying areas. Further demolition is planned in the heart of Rothwell including St Georges Hospital, only opened in 1904 and now earmarked for redevelopment. When the older generation has gone who will remain to be nostalgic about old Rothwell and to remind future generations of their heritage? We feel sure that the community should look to its future. However, this does not mean the past must be forgotten. With this book we have tried to record the heritage of our community, giving older residents the opportunity to enjoy a journey down memory lane and allowing younger residents and future generations to discover their roots.

Simon Bulmer and Albert Brown
May 1999

One
Pits and Coal Mining

Rose Pit situated on the pastures of Rothwell Haigh, c. 1900. The existence of the pit was first recorded in 1846 and it was working in 1850. According to Batty it was so named because of the profusion of wild roses in the area. The last coal was extracted in the 1920s, however it was subsequently used as a winding shaft for men and supplies.

A more rural look towards Rose Pit, *c*. 1900. This was before waste covered half of the pastures as happened in later years.

A view of the East and West Union Junction Railway showing coal wagons on the Rose Pit sidings, *c*. 1918.

Rear of Beeston Pit, *c.* 1910. This is Deputies Row showing Mr Harold Kempshall and friends.

Beeston Bed Pit was sunk in 1892. This pit didn't reopen after the miners' strike of 1926. After that time the coal from this pit came out to the surface via Fanny Pit.

Deputies Row and other houses on the A61 Leeds to Wakefield Road at the top of Bell Hill, *c*. 1910. The gates to Beeston Pit yard are clearly shown on the right.

The coal screens of Beeston Pit, *c*. 1960. These were installed during the mine workers strike of 1926 but never used.

Pictured from the right, in 1902, are: head carpenter and wheelwright, William Hartley, who worked at Low Shops until eighty years of age; his grandson, Hartley Banks and nephew, Joseph Chadwick. They were responsible for all woodwork at Low Shops and were resident joiners at all other J. & J. Charlesworths Pits in the area.

A group of fitters stand by the main beam of the 'New Engine', at J. & J. Charlesworths Low Shops, c. 1909.

It is hard to realise in these days of automated and semi-automated coal mining that only half a lifetime ago there was next to no mechanisation. The work was done by shire horses. This is why a well manned shoeing forge and farriers shop were vital requirements. In 1924 there were 24 shire horses stabled at Beeston Pit. 160 ponies were stabled underground at Fanny Pit in 1922, less than 10 years later there were only 20 ponies stabled there.

One of J. & J. Charlesworths steam locomotives, most of which were built locally. This particular picture is at Low Shops sidings with Hunslet and District workhouse in the background.

Number 9 engine at Low Shops, *c.* 1910. It was still working twenty-five years later at Fanny Pit.

The sinking of Fanny Pit shaft, *c.* 1911. The winding engine house is still under construction on the right, with the boilers used for steam power just visible.

Mr Ingham stokes the Lancashire boilers to provide steam power during the construction of Fanny Pit, *c.* 1910.

Surface workers at the Fanny Pit are pictured outside the pay office in 1911.

Mr Harold Earl (on the right) and a workmate, outside Fanny Pit tippler house, c. 1955. The tipper house on the right was where the coal came from the drift, in the wagons, and was tipped onto a conveyor belt to be taken for washing.

Miners are pictured collecting their wage tally from the first window, enabling them to draw their wages, from the wages clerk, at the next window, *c.* 1950. The four men on the right are, from the right: Les Fox, Albert Peat, Reg Share and Joe Cochrane.

Fanny Pit yard, with underground workers coming off the day shift in the 1950s.

In 1922 a new upcast shaft was sunk at Fanny Pit to improve the underground ventilation. The old Midland shaft remained a ventilation shaft until after the sinking was completed.

Surface workers pose for a photograph during the sinking of a new shaft at Fanny Pit.

A gathering of workers who were employed in the sinking of a new shaft at Fanny Pit. The young man at the front is showing the signals board, this indicated the rules for lowering and raising the tub or hoppett.

Harry Earl and Laurie Dunwell (lamproom foreman) are pictured in the lamproom at Fanny Pit, *c.* 1958.

Stuart Earl drives locomotive 719 at Fanny Pit bottom. This view is taken in the man riding station with the locomotive ready to take a full load of miners to the coal face; it was known in the pit as the miners Paddy. This locomotive is now on view at the Midland Railway Centre in Derbyshire.

An aerial view of Fanny Pit, c. 1978.

A Collins Miner unmanned machine, c. 1965. This was used in Fanny Pit for cutting new coal faces.

Armitages stone quarry at Thorpe.

Armitages stone quarry, showing just how deep the workings had become.

One of the processes which took place prior to the stone being cut.

Polishing the stone to a fine finish.

Machine cut stone waits to be finished.

This stone mill is on the A61 Leeds to Wakefield Road at Robin Hood. It was built in the 1840s for cutting and finishing the stone.

Two

Churches, Chapels and Religion

An Ineson postcard showing Lofthouse cemetery, c. 1910.

This Ineson postcard looks from Springhead Park towards Rothwell vicarage on what was Woodlesford Lane, now Park Lane, c. 1908.

Rothwell Parish Church and Lych Gate.

Rothwell parish church in 1905. The dwelling on the right is said to have been the house of Levi Barker who made clogs for miners at two shillings and sixpence a pair.

A interior view of Rothwell parish church looking from the font towards the altar. The nineteenth-century carvings at the end of each pew are a unique feature.

East view of Rothwell parish church, c. 1950.

South view of Rothwell parish church showing the 1880 extensions, *c.* 1950. Also pictured are the old tombstones as they were before the clearance of the front of the church.

A view showing clearly how close the burials were at the front of Rothwell parish church, *c.* 1950.

Main entrance to Rothwell
vicarage, which was built in the
late nineteenth century.

The rear of Rothwell vicarage is seen from what was Woodlesford Lane. This was first occupied
by the Reverend E. Heberden, who was vicar of Rothwell from 1872 to 1882.

A view of the entrance to Ouzlewell Green Wesleyan Methodists chapel. This was converted out of two cottages in the nineteenth century and replaced the earlier wooden chapel situated on the opposite side of the road.

In the early days of Methodism at Rothwell, services were held in a stable in Butcher Lane belonging to Mr North, a well-to-do farmer. After his death the property and land were conveyed to thirteen trustees of the Methodist faith by John North's widow and eldest son, for five shillings. John Wesley preached in this chapel in 1772. The later chapel, opened in 1880, was enlarged and altered over the years.

Lofthouse Wesleyan chapel, *c.* 1950. The chapel is situated on the A61 Leeds to Wakefield Road, it was built in 1840 and enlarged in 1870.

A view from Marsh Street of the Primitive Methodist chapel. It was built in 1874 to replace the Ebenezer chapel off Commercial Street. Joseph Priestley College now occupies the site.

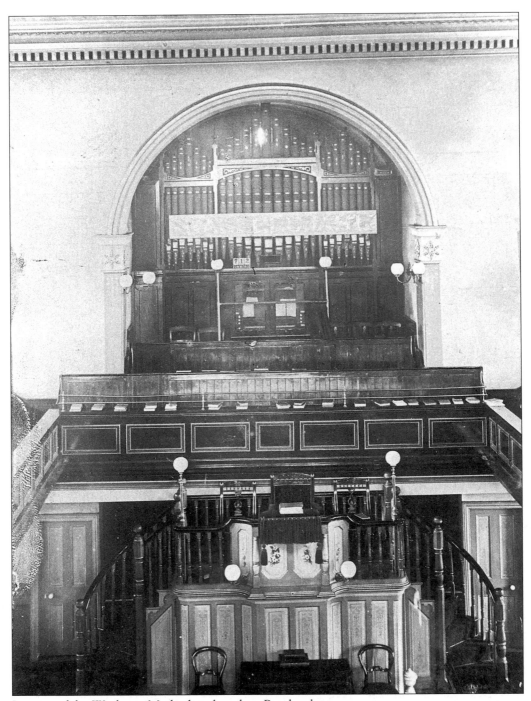

Interior of the Wesleyan Methodist chapel on Butcher lane.

Matt Ward's shop was situated at the bottom of Hargreaves Street. The horse-drawn flat cart carried the Sunday school organ and attendant musicians, which always led the chapel procession. This was an annual event held on Whit Sunday.

Open-air service. This was part of the Whit Sunday walk celebration at Lofthouse.

A carved stone head, pictured in 1998. This is one of many to be found on the four pinnacles at the top of Rothwell parish church tower. These date back to 1877 when Thomas Stainer, mason, was given the job of reconstructing the four pinnacles because of their poor state of decay.

A view of Rothwell parish church from the end of Ingram Parade, with Shaw Ditch on the left.

Robin Hood chapel on the north side of Sharp Lane.

Stourton Methodist chapel.

Carlton Wesleyan Methodist church in Chapel Street, *c.* 1900.

St Andrews church on Pontefract Road, Stourton. It was built around 1900, replacing the tin chapel Mission.

One of the entrances to Oulton Hall with the spire of Oulton church in the distance, c. 1900.

An Ineson postcard of Oulton church, built in 1829.

Ebenezer chapel, off Commercial Street. It was constructed because of a disagreement between two factions within the membership of the Wesleyan Methodist chapel, in Butcher Lane. This split led to the breakaway sect calling themselves Primitive Methodists. It was this sect that built the Ebenezer chapel around 1818 by voluntary subscription or labour. They were known locally as 'The Ranters'.

Three
Commercial Street

Commercial Street ends at the junction with Gillett Lane and Oulton Lane. This scene shows the Empire Picture house, built in 1912, which commenced showing silent films in 1913. Also pictured is the terminus of the Rothwell to Leeds tram route.

The junction of Marsh Street and Commercial Street, previously called Town Street. It shows Albert Ward's corner shop, selling groceries and occasional hardware. It was demolished after the Second World War to allow for the widening to the entrance to Marsh Street.

The north side of Commercial Street, opposite Albert Ward's shop, showing Mr Shearman's hardware shop. This was built in 1899, replacing an ancient property belonging to Tom Shearman, which housed the Black Bull Hotel, offices, shop and dwellings. This view looks past Shearman's shop down Commercial Street past West Parade and towards the Coach and Horses public house.

An Ineson postcard of the south view of Commercial Street showing Charles Ineson's post office-come-drapers shop. Charles Ineson was also a printer and published picture postcard views of Rothwell and surrounding areas. This postcard is dated 1908. Note the entrance of the ginnel – an ancient right of way from Commercial Street (Town Street) into Marsh Street.

An updated version of Ineson's 1908 picture postcard.

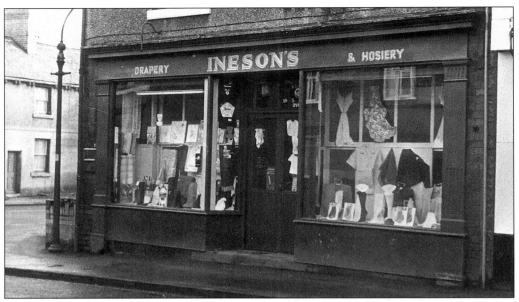

Ineson's shop, *c.* 1940. The post office closed in 1916 leaving only the drapers and hosiery business.

This scene was captured during the celebrations for the Jubilee of George V and Queen Mary in 1935. Mr Frankland's barber shop can be seen on the left.

John Elstop's; chemist, druggist and retailer of petroleum. John Elstob was the secretary of the private social welfare club, which provided a week long holiday at Scarborough for five shillings a week – but the patients had to take their own soap and towel.

A modern view of the Coach and Horses public house. This building post-dates the single-storey thatched house. It was purchased by Mr Calverley, Lord of the Manor, in the second half of the nineteenth century at which time it became the meeting place of Rothwell manor court.

The entrance to jail yard was once a common right of way into the tofts and crofts of Rothwell Haigh, seen here around 1950.

Three old cottages in Commercial Street which were, at the beginning of the century, Nos 36, 38 and 40. The property as a whole was built originally, around 1610, as a gentleman's private residence. It is now a listed building and contains an ornate seventeenth-century plaster ceiling.

Local boys compare their bikes in Commercial Street.

Commercial Street, looking back towards the Black Bull Hotel. On the left of the picture are the ancient back-to-back cottages, these were demolished in the 1920s to make way for the Midland Bank building. The first cottage exhibits the barber's pole of Arthur Sunderland's barber shop. This was where the first telephone exchange was installed in the 1880s.

The middle of Commercial Street, showing the Halifax building society premises which was formerly the Miners Arms public house. At the end of Meynell Avenue is the building which accommodated the old shop of Sam Heaton, butcher. The site is now occupied by a modern precinct.

Rothwell registrar's office and a dwelling are pictured next to Charles Wards the grocer. This was at the time of the Coronation of Edward VII in 1902. The building now forms the premises of Elmsley's solicitors and Boots the Chemists.

Charles Ward family grocers shop was established in 1866. They sold, at the turn of the century, washing machines for three shillings – or three shillings and sixpence delivered.

A further view of Charles Ward's shop, together with Harry Edwards – fruitier and wet fish merchant.

The cottages in Commercial Street stand on the east side of the entrance to the gasworks yard. These premises belonged to the Copley family in the eighteenth and nineteenth centuries. It was discovered during their demolition that the buildings were much older than expected, as sixteenth-century pargeting was found after the removal of the eighteenth-century brick casing.

This scene from the time of the building's demolition clearly shows the ornate sixteenth-century pargeting.

On the left is the former *Rothwell Times* newspaper office, at this time (*c.* 1950) the building housed Armitage and Rawling printers. To the right hand side is the wall of the old Rothwell church school, now part of Morrison's supermarket.

This building was once stated to be the finest example of an Elizabethan gentleman's residence. In the eighteenth century it was owned by Sir William Lowther of Swillington Hall. It was rebuilt by Mr Holmes in the nineteenth century.

Queen Victoria's Jubilee celebrations in 1897. Alfred Drew, grocer, and his family are pictured outside his shop. On the right is the Hare and Hounds public house, Richard Rodley's boot and shoe makers shop is on the left. The first trainload of goods into Rothwell station included a consignment of flour for Mr Drew. This was loaded onto a decorated wagon and paraded around Rothwell headed by two Rothwell bands.

Andrew Marshall and staff of the *Rothwell Times* pose to celebrate the newspaper's tenth anniversary in 1883.

The end of Commercial Street, showing the market cross with lion house to the rear. The little girl shown standing with her mother grew up to become Mrs Robinson – the owner of this photograph. They stand outside the house that was at one time Nanny Stead's Dame school.

Pottery Fold off the top of Mill Hill. This was built to house the workers of Rothwell pottery which began production in the eighteenth century.

Standing outside Lion House, looking down Mill Hill towards the parish church.

This ornate Jacobean ceiling, from around 1610, is still to be seen today in the shop on Commercial Street.

A wintry scene dominated by the old market cross. This was erected after the right to a weekly market was granted by King Henry IV in 1408. Rose Pit can be seen on the horizon.

Four

Business and Industry

This postcard from the Cycle series was published in the *Yorkshire Evening News*. It shows the quiet Leeds to Barnsdale road and the John O Gaunt Hotel. This was built after the construction of the Turnpike Road in 1820 by James Verity (Stonemason) who also build the present day Black Bull public house, in Commercial Street.

Edward Wright, wheelwright of Spibey Lane. He began to repair gypsy caravans from the middle of the nineteenth century. Later he produced his own type of caravan called a Yorkshire Bow which had a canvas top. His sons carried on the tradition of caravan building into the 1920s.

A Yorkshire Bow caravan made by the Wrights.

A recent photograph, at Thwaite Mills, of a Yorkshire Bow built by Wright's of Rothwell.

The fine detail that the Wrights incorporated into their caravans is clearly illustrated here.

The Wrights produced other designs of caravan, this is the Reading type.

The tram terminus outside the Black Bull Hotel. The building pictured on the right was eventually converted into houses, though it started life as a dance hall and also had a period of use as a slaughterhouse.

An ancient building on the junction of Commercial Street and Cross Street. It is seen in 1935 prior to its demolition. In 1893 it was the ILP (Independent Labour Party) Club.

The Anchor Inn at the side of the Aire and Calder Navigation. It stood at the bottom of Bullock Lane next to the lock house. The inn belonged to the Craven family around the turn of the century.

The rear of the ancient corn mill and dam. Some clue is given to its location as we can see Rothwell parish church in the background. The mill was valued in the Domesday Book at two shillings per annum.

A further view of the mill and dam.

From the bottom of Mill Hill we are looking into the corn mill yard with the footbridge over the overflow at the entry into the ford.

The ford through the River Dolphin from the mill yard.

This is believed to be Mr Wilcock, mill labourer, pictured while loading flour sacks in the old corn mill.

A view of the goit channelling the water from the mill wheel into Rothwell beck.

A side view of Thwaite Mills, which started life as a corn mill though later on it was used to grind flint. It is now run as a museum by Leeds City Council.

Derelict Fleet Mills at Fleet Oulton. Records show that the mill was in existence in the fifteenth century. In 1926 a devastating fire gutted the mill and it never reopened.

A view of Fleet Mills taken from the River Aire. This also shows a small part of the lost village of Fleet.

This shows how extensive an area Fleet Mill covered.

This tea pot was produced locally.

An example of a drinking vessel that was also produced locally.

A further example of local pottery.

A pewter tankard of John of Gaunt's time which was discovered in the old Rothwell manor house.

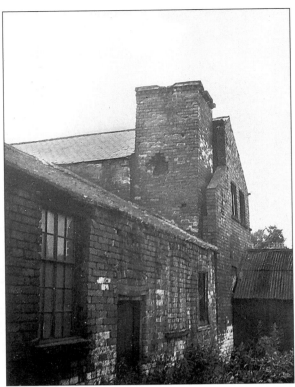

One of the outbuildings belonging to Rothwell match works. Originally this was opened near the goit in 1840. In 1875 after several fires, the match works was rebuilt, this time using brick and iron sheeting. The chimney shown here was used in the process of drying the match heads. The final year of production of matches on this site was 1902.

Outhouses at Rothwell match works were kept apart to reduce the risk of fires spreading.

This was known as Carlton Bridge Brewery though in fact it never brewed beer. After its construction Bentleys Brewery purchased the building from William Nichols to prevent any competition. Later it was converted to stabling for Messrs J. & J. Charlesworths' horses.

A view of Gurling-stones yards on Pontefract Road. This was started during the coal strike of 1926 to provide employment for out of work miners by Mr Gurling. It provided pre-cast concrete products.

Oulton Hall Home Farm. This is believed to have been built in the sixteenth century.

When Lofthouse Pit was in production this old property was covered over with waste. It was locally known as Lofthouse Manor Farm.

Wallice Arnold's petrol station on the Leeds to Wakefield road at Stourton. Pictured are Stourton petrol station showing Enid Higgins, pump attendant, with her younger sister Hazel in the mid-1950s.

An artistic view of Rothwell Manor Farm as seen from the pastures. It is said that stone from Rothwell Castle was reused, by Roger Hopton, to build this manor house.

This view of Manor House clearly shows much of the original timber frame. It was built in 1486 by Roger Hopton, constable of Pontefract Castle.

A rural view of the mill pond on Rothwell pastures. In the background are Rothwell parish church and Manor House together with the medieval grouting of what is said to be John of Gaunt's chapel.

South door of Rothwell Manor House.
The older medieval part of the house is
on the left and the eighteenth-century
wing on the right.

This unfortunate scene is
of the old Manor House's
demolition in the 1970s.
The timber frame was
taken into storage by West
Yorkshire Archaeological
Service where it remains
today.

The old manor house was demolished because it was judged to be structurally unsafe.

This is believed to be the great barn of Rothwell Manor house, built in the eighteenth century.

Five

Transport

The old toll house at the bottom of Sharp Lane on the Leeds to Wakefield Road. It was built around 1753 following the construction of the Leeds-Wakefield turnpike road. Travellers would have to pay at each toll house to be able to use the road.

An Ineson postcard showing Rothwell Station. This property was not built until passenger services were projected. A luncheon was held for shareholders of the East & West Junction Railway and the newly formed South Leeds Railways in 1904.

Rothwell Station, looking in an easterly direction.

In connection with the promotion of Rothwell's passenger railway, a row of houses for railway workers was built in Wood Lane, together with a handsome new house for the railway superintendent. This was later extended to form the Liberal Club and then Rothwell Parish Hall.

This excavator of an American design called 'American Devil' was capable of doing the work of fifty men. Here we see work carried out during construction of the East and West Junction Railway in 1880.

Railway Bridge.

This railway was laid down in 1838 and was first known as the Leeds to Derby Railway. At the time of this photograph Messrs Bentleys' gas plant was situated on the west side of the road opposite the main entrance to the brewery (near the distant horse and cart).

Empty coal wagons on Woodlesford sidings. Further on is Woodlesford station.

A barge carries coal on the Aire and Calder Navigation.

This barge is pulling 'Tom Puddings'. These were large metal boxes for the transportation of coal on the Aire and Calder Navigation.

A coal-carrying sailing barge. This picture was taken outside the Anchor Inn, Rothwell.

A tug heads off to collect its cargo.

Mr Craven is pictured on his Douglas motorbike, outside the Anchor Inn. The lock-keepers house is in the background.

A Leyland solid-tyred charabanc. This type of vehicle could be converted to a lorry by replacing the seating area with a trailer bed. Richard Fox is thought to be in the driving seat.

Note that the speed at which the charabanc might travel was only twelve miles per hour.

Richard Fox show off their new single-decker bus, in the early 1920s. It was used as a transport service bus, travelling from Wakefield to Leeds via Rothwell.

Edward Brothers' Swillington service bus stands at Rothwell cenotaph, at the junction of Gillett Lane, Commercial Street and Oulton Lane in the 1920s.

Newton & Wards bus. This ran in direct competition with R. Fox's bus service from Wakefield to Leeds. It is shown here in Swingate outside the tram sheds.

Thatched Cottages, Lofthouse.

On the left are the old thatched cottages on the Leeds to Wakefield road, at Lofthouse. An open-top tram makes its way to Leeds, *c.* 1900.

This tram is on its way to Wakefield from Lofthouse Lane end. The Rose and Crown Hotel stands on the corner.

No. 25 – one of the early double-decker, open-topped electric trams. It is pictured at the top of Bell Hill, at the junction with Wood Lane.

No. 3 tram stands at the junction of Meynell Avenue and Ingram Parade.

Tramcar at the junction of Wood Lane, Spibey Lane and Haigh Road. It is on its way to the Rothwell terminus outside the Black Bull Hotel on Commercial Street. Even today, the scene seems little changed.

88

Richard Fox in Meynell Avenue, he built the house and premises in 1899. He ran a horse and carriage service for weddings and funerals.

Horse-drawn carriage was the means of transport for this well-to-do family.

This is believed to be Mr Hutchinson, with his donkey cart and a family from Rothwell.

Miss Turner poses with a penny-farthing bicycle.

This couple, pictured in their car, is believed to be Mr and Mrs Armitage.

This picture reflects the rural nature of upper Royds Lane, *c.* 1910. The lane was once part of the King's highway between Leeds and Pontefract, in the days before turnpike roads.

Mr Kemshall, in his motor car, is parked outside a garage in Meynell Avenue.

Sam Ward is in his car outside his father's grocers shop on the corner of Commercial Street and Marsh Street.

This car is outside what was, in 1916, Rothwell's post office in Commercial Street.

This steam engine was made locally and is pictured outside the John O Gaunt Hotel, at the end of the First World War.

Six

Leisure

A typical middle-class Victorian parlour. The Victorians liked their homes full of ornaments and pictures.

Rothwell children's home, on Wood Lane. These girls are pictured in their school housewifery class. Note the teacher showing the girls how to cook.

Rothwell Bowling Green Hotel (locally known as 'The Rabbit Trap'), *c.* 1944.

An Ineson postcard of Rothwell, *c.* 1900. This is a rural scene of the parish church, Manor House and ruined castle. Mr Basil Abbishaw, Tom Brook and Tom Barret are believed to be the people on the punt.

Robin Hood Pit officials, *c.* 1912.

Oulton Girls Friendly Society at the turn of the century.

These children are dressed up for the White Garland, in 1905. It is thought that the children were from the Rothwell church school.

This group of young ladies are believed to be posing in Springhead Park.

Rothwell Angling club. The man in shirt-sleeves may be Ben Taylor, the landlord of the Bowling Green Hotel.

This scene in Springhead Park was taken on Infirmary Sunday, when local brass bands would play selections of music and make a collection on behalf of the Leeds Infirmary. In the foreground, partly obscured by the contour of the land, is part of the great carriage driveway through the park from the main gates in Oulton Lane. In those days Springhead Park was only a small part of what is now Rothwell Park. The rest of the park at that time was subdivided into fields.

A close up view of HMS *Springhead* on the beck, in 1895

This is believed to be Carlton cricket team.

The bowling club members, based at the Bowling Green Hotel.

Springhead Park in the 1930s. Springhead Park was originally privately owned, but came into the hands of Rothwell Urban District Council in the 1930s.

Tennis courts, café and bowling green in Springhead Park in the 1930s.

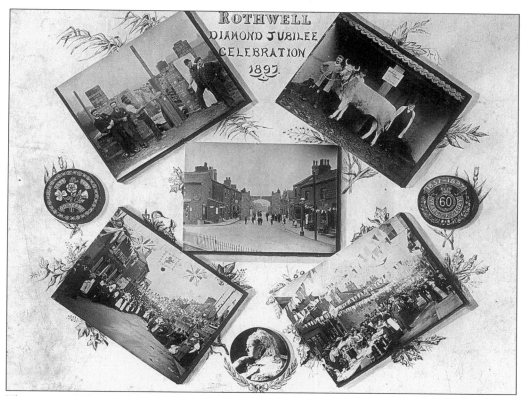

This group of photographs celebrates the Diamond Jubilee of Queen Victoria in 1897.

End of Commercial Street, showing the triumphal arch. This was also known as the 'Bread Arch' because people were given parcels of food left over from the previous day's celebrations. On the far right are the old premises of Tom Shearman, these were used prior to the newer building that can be seen today.

A further photograph from the time of Queen Victoria's Diamond Jubilee. This shows the steer that was bought at Wakefield to be killed and roasted for the celebration.

The celebrations continue. The steer has now been killed and is being roasted. The location of the roasting was Whitehall Garth, between the Black Bull Hotel and Whitehall Farm, just off Commercial Street.

A street party is underway in Commercial Street, near the Hare and Hounds public house, in celebration of the Diamond Jubilee.

The Ineson family stand outside their shop on Commercial Street, next to the Triumphal Arch. The post office is on the left with Mr Ineson's printing shop on the right; it later become a drapery shop.

Mr Jack Brown outside his sweet and tobacconists shop in Commercial Street. Previously these premises had been an apothecary shop. This view shows another royal celebration – this time the Coronation of Edward VII in 1902.

This is thought to be a visit to Scarborough for the family of Tom Collins, who was the senior deputy of Fanny Pit.

Christmas day in the workhouse in 1904. This is in the main dinning hall of Rothwell Workhouse, now St Georges Hospital.

Rothwell carnival passes along Marsh Street, *c.* 1912.

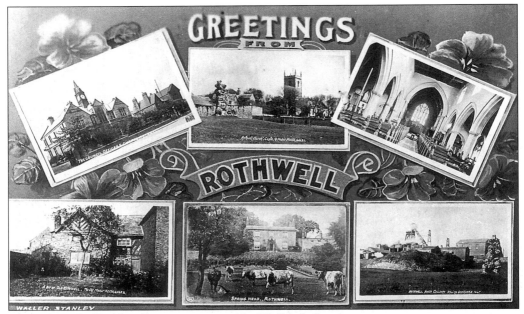

This postcard of Rothwell views was issued by Waller & Stanley.

Mr Hartley lays the foundation stone for Carlton Temperance Society at the turn of the century.

Members of Rothwell Model Brass Band in the late nineteenth century.

Rothwell Temperance Band, pictured in their Lancers uniforms in 1883.

Rothwell Temperance Band, *c.* 1945.

Shay Fields at Carlton, this was once one of the common fields of Carlton.

'The Nookin'. The date on the cross-beam reads 1611 but it is believed to be much older than that.

Some of the residents of East View, Woodlesford enjoy the sunshine and celebrations for the Silver Jubilee of Queen Elizabeth II, in 1977.

Rothwell Urban District Council members are pictured at the formation of the council in 1895.

Rothwell Parks Bowling Club, 1944.

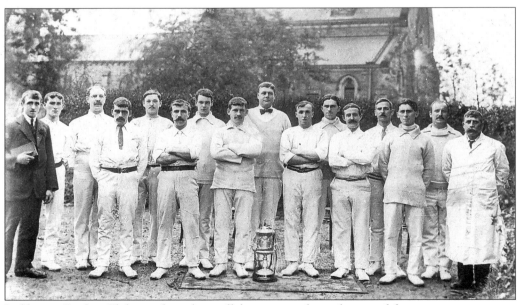

Lofthouse Cricket Club members show off their cup in the early part of the century.

Seven
Buildings

The Calverley family of Oulton Hall. Lords of the Manor of Oulton have lived in the village for many generations. This is the 1855 hall, which was rebuilt after the great fire that destroyed the earlier hall.

In the yard of Rothwell debtors gaol. This shows the extension that was added to the gaol around 1700.

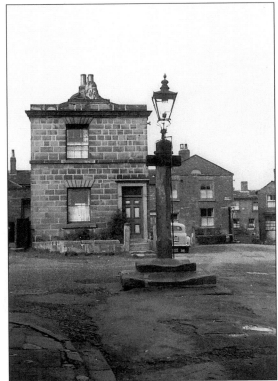

Lion House at the cross end of Commercial Street. This was built in the place of an old cottage in 1854.

The Ida's at Stourton, off Pontefract Road. This is yet another example of a lost village, like Fleet at Oulton, Stourton, which has disappeared.

A postcard view of The Rothwell Urban District Council offices in Marsh Street.

This building was a smallpox hospital in the 1880s. It was rented by Rothwell Local Health Board for three shillings and sixpence per week from Mrs Beeton. She was allowed to live in the property as caretaker at sixpence per week.

Rothwell Liberal Club on Wood Lane.

A further view of Lion House. It stands alone on the site, as demolition of other buildings goes on all around.

These workmen are assembled outside the local Highways Depot of the Rothwell Urban District Council at Lofthouse, near to Rodillian School.

Rothwell council offices, seen from Springfield Street. The Marsh, until its enclosure in 1809, was called the waste of Rothwell.

Looking down Oulton Lane from Commercial Street, the Hargreaves motor transport depot can be seen in the distance.

Offices and waiting room of the Wakefield Electric Tramway Company, now Pelican Engineering, on the Leeds to Wakefield road. The building on the right is the conversion house where 33,000 volts of electricity came from the grid to be converted into a workable current for the tramway company.

The last remnant of Rothwell Royal Hunting Lodge or castle. The pillar of grouting is claimed to be part of the fourteenth-century John of Gaunt's chapel. It was recorded contemporaneously by Thoresby, as one of two grouting pillars said to be the remnants of the castle chapel.

An old malt kiln on West Field Road Carlton used for processing malt which was used by the brewing industry. An old beam inside the building dates the structure to 1772.

Locally known as Cheesecake House this cottage is believed to have been built on the Wakefield Turnpike Road in the seventeenth century.

Oulton Hall Home Farm.

Rothwell Isolation Hospital, Haigh Road, built in 1901. It was here that patients with consumption were treated in special open fronted wards.

Rothwell parish church common Hurst House, *c.* 1946. Poorer people could hire the hurst for one shilling.

Old cottages and the Three Horse Shoes Inn at the end of Green Bottom Road, now St Johns Street, in Oulton.

The new precinct before Morrisons was built. Looking towards the Methodist chapel on Butcher Lane.

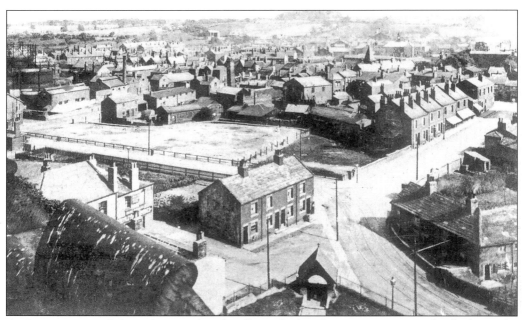

An Ineson postcard, from the top of Rothwell parish church tower, c. 1904. It clearly shows the centre of Rothwell as it was at the beginning of this century.

A slightly later view of Rothwell from the church, *c.* 1907. The area is already showing signs of further development and there is a local tram on the corner of Meynell Avenue and Church Street.

Moving on another twenty-three years to 1930. This shows further evidence of how much Rothwell was changing.

Bringing the scene up to date, to 1998, some ninety-four years since the first shot. This clearly illustrates that Rothwell has changed considerably in the intervening decades.

This house on the junction of Marsh Street and Butcher Lane dates back to the late eighteenth century yet even today remains easily recognizable.